Girls Got Game

girls' **SKATEBOARDING**

Skating to Be the Best

by Terri Dougherty

Consultant
Action Sports Alliance, Inc., "The Alliance"
Drew Mearns, Executive Director and Co-Founder,
CB Burnside, President and Co-Founder,
and Mimi Knoop, Co-Founder

Capstone press®

Mankato, Minnesota

Snap Books are published by Capstone Press,
151 Good Counsel Drive, P.O. Box 669, Mankato, Minnesota 56002.
www.capstonepress.com

Library of Congress Cataloging-in-Publication Data
Dougherty, Terri.
    Girls' skateboarding: skating to be the best / by Terri Dougherty.
    p. cm.—(Snap books. Girls got game)
    Summary: "Describes girls' skateboarding, including equipment,
basic moves, and famous professionals in the sport"—Provided by publisher.
    Includes bibliographical references and index.
    ISBN-13: 978-1-4296-0134-4 (hardcover)
    ISBN-10: 1-4296-0134-5 (hardcover)
    1. Skateboarding—Juvenile literature. 2. Sports for women—Juvenile literature.
I. Title. II. Series.
GV859.8.D68 2008
796.22082—dc22   2007002484

Editors: Kendra Christensen and Jennifer Besel
Designer: Bobbi J. Wyss
Photo Researchers: Charlene Deyle and Scott Thoms

Photo Credits:
AP/Wide World Photos/Jae C. Hong, 23; Capstone Press/Karon Dubke, back cover, 10, 11, 13, 14, 15 (all), 18–19, 20–21; Corbis/NewSport/
Steve Boyle, 27; Glen E. Friedman, 8; MRZPHOTO, cover, 5, 7, 17, 25, 26, 28, 29; Photo courtesy of Terri Dougherty, 32; Zuma Press/
Pierre Tostee, 9

Capstone Press thanks Jamie Erickson and the YMCA Chesley Skate Park in Mankato, Minnesota, for their assistance with this book.
Capstone Press also thanks Peggy Oki for her assistance with the book. Peggy's website is http://www.peggy-oki.com.

1 2 3 4 5 6 12 11 10 09 08 07

TABLE OF CONTENTS

ON THE EDGE

There's something edgy and exciting about skateboarding. Maybe it's seeing a girl catch big air or grind down a rail. That definitely demands attention!

Skateboarding is cool and fun, and it's not just for guys. Girls are skateboarding and loving it. They're tackling street and ramp style skating and having a great time.

There's no reason you can't skateboard too. Get on your board in the driveway and learn to balance. Head to the skatepark with your friends. You'll be carving around the bowl in no time!

Lyn-Z Adams
Hawkins

Part of the Crowd

Girls look cool and confident at the skatepark. They're taking turns dropping into the bowl and showing their best tricks in contests.

Skateboarding is really not about competition, though. It's a sport that's mainly just meant to be enjoyed. You can skate the streets, doing grinds and tricks in street skating. Or you can wow everyone by skating ramps and bowls in vert skating.

One of the best parts of being a skateboarder is making friends with people who love the sport too. When you have a skateboard, you have something in common with all the other skaters out there. You're part of one of the most adventurous crowds around.

" Believe in yourself and go for it—in whatever you like to do. And don't listen to the naysayers.
—Mimi Knoop,
X Games
skateboarding medalist "

Nicole Zuck

Skating through History

It didn't matter to Peggy Oki that there were no other girls on the Zephyr skateboard team in the 1970s. She skated in Dogtown, in Santa Monica, California, where guys were doing surfing moves on skateboards. She loved to skate so much that she didn't even think about being the only girl on the team.

Peggy Oki

Amy
Caron

The Dogtown skateboarders took their style of skating to school playgrounds and empty swimming pools. Their moves laid the groundwork for trick skaters like Jen O'Brien to catch a frontside air at the X Games. This popular event hosts one of the biggest skateboarding competitions in the world. On the street skating side, Lauren Perkins, Marissa Del Santo, and Amy Caron are doing backside 50-50 grinds and frontside boardslides as they pave the way for skaters like you!

CHAPTER TWO

YOU AND THE BOARD

Interested in grinding like the pros? Well, the only way to learn is to get on your board. Stay positive as you learn to balance and roll. It won't be easy. But with practice and persistence, you'll be skating in no time.

You don't have to learn alone either. Some skateparks offer lessons for beginners. Watching and talking with other skaters is a great way to pick up some tips too.

And remember, you can practice anywhere. Almost any place where there isn't a lot of traffic is a great place to practice! But before you can start practicing, you'll need to get the right gear.

Getting on Board

Skateboards are not one-size-fits-all. Picking out a board that works for you is one key to success. Decks, wheels, and trucks are all built for different types of skating. If your goal is to do flip tricks and grinds, you'll want a small deck to stand on and small, light wheels. If speed is your need, grab a wide board and large wheels. Ask the people at your skate shop to help you get just the right board.

Pads and a helmet should also be part of your skateboard gear. Knee and elbow pads cut down on bumps and bruises. Your helmet should be made for skateboarding so it can withstand the impacts that can come with the sport.

To give yourself the best chance of staying on top of the skateboard, wear skateboard shoes. They're wide and have flat soles. To make sure they don't wear out right away, they should be reinforced. As a bonus, they look cool!

Deck

Wheel

Truck

Learn the Basics

Now that you've got your gear, it's time to get rolling. Start by learning how to stand on the board. Put your feet parallel on the board. Regular stance is when your left foot is at the front. But if that doesn't feel right, you can skate goofyfoot, with your right foot in front. Once you have the feel of the board, try giving yourself a push with your back foot. Tilt the board from side to side as you're rolling to get a good balance.

Then it's time to learn the backbone of all skating tricks, the ollie. This trick isn't easy, but you've got to learn it if you want to do any other airborne stunt.

1. Put your back foot at the end of the board and your front foot in the middle.

2. From a bent position, jump up, snap the back of the board on the ground, and pull your front foot toward the front of the board all at once.

3. Use your front foot to level out the board while you're in flight.

 Yeah, it's hard at first, even the guys tumble around. But the payoff is that it feels good when those guys come back to the park and they're like, 'Whoa!'

—CB Burnside,
X Games skateboarding medalist

CHAPTER THREE

DROPPING IN ANYWHERE

You might think that finding time to practice skating will be hard. But actually you can practice all the time. The skateboard is a great means of transportation. You can skate to school, to your friend's house, and anywhere the sidewalk will take you.

Why not skate to the skatepark? Many cities have outdoor skateparks where you can practice your moves and meet other skaters. There are ramps and street obstacles like curbs and rails. Some cities have indoor skateparks, where you don't have to worry about the weather ruining your session.

Make your trip to the skatepark even more fun by bringing some friends along or meeting them there. With tricks to try and skateboarders to watch, you'll have lots to talk about.

Mimi
Knoop

Skatepark Etiquette

Even though there are no rules to skateboarding, there are some unwritten guidelines at the skatepark. Not everyone can drop into the bowl at the same time. That would be mass confusion and result in a lot of injuries.

To keep things from getting out of control, skateboarders usually form an unofficial order. Someone puts their board over the lip of the bowl and is ready to go. Other skaters notice and let the skater in. You'll learn these unwritten rules by hanging out with other skaters.

Start at the Bottom

Dropping in on the vert ramp for the first time can be scary. Pro skateboarder Mimi Knoop suggests starting at the bottom. Use kickturns, a trick that has you turning the board on one set of wheels, to help you get to the top. That might help you get comfortable with the height. Once you feel ready, you can drop in from the top.

Practice Makes Perfect

No one is born a top skater. You are going to have to practice a lot! Challenge yourself to skate in new places. If the local skatepark is getting ho-hum, check out one in a nearby city.

As you become more experienced, dare yourself to learn new tricks, like grinds or aerials. Be creative and see if you can string a few together to make it interesting.

And yes, you will become great at falling too. Don't get discouraged. Not even the pros land every trick every time. The best skateboarders set themselves apart by trying until they finally get it. They even fall in competitions, because they're not afraid to challenge themselves to be the best.

Fall the Right Way

Did you know there's a right way to fall? Knowing how to fall can help keep you from getting hurt.

- When you're losing your balance, crouch down so you won't fall as hard.

- Land on your rear or side to save your wrists and elbows.

- When you land, roll diagonally from one shoulder to the opposite hip, to lessen the impact.

CHAPTER FOUR

SKATING TO THE TOP

Now that you've practiced and practiced, you're ready for some recognition. Contests are sponsored by skateboard companies at local skateparks. Find out about them by asking around at your skate shop, or you can search the Internet for contests in your area.

Before you drop in on a contest, have a variety of tricks ready. In a contest, girls often skate in jam session format. They all wait around the bowl and take turns showing their best tricks.

Once you're really good, you can move on to national contests. They are held all over the United States and Canada. The best skaters are invited to the X Games.

The Alliance

A group of female skateboarders called The Alliance wants to take women's skateboarding to the next level. They want to encourage more girls to get into skateboarding and hope to sponsor more national contests for women. They're also looking to increase the prize money given to female skateboard contest winners.

CB Burnside

In the Judge's Eyes

At contests, judges take notes as they check out the difficulty level of the tricks. A skater landing a kickflip indy is very impressive! They watch to see if the skaters are linking a couple good runs together and note how many tricks are landed. Being inconsistent, by falling or bailing out of a trick, will bring a score down.

Judges give good scores when a skateboarder gets big air above the ramp. They also want to see some tricks on the lip of the bowl. Some of the scoring is based on a judge's gut opinion. They watch to see how much style a girl puts into her runs. At the end of the contest, the judges compare scores and name a winner.

Get Rewarded for Skating

Some of the top skateboarders are fortunate enough to have sponsors. These sponsors pay for the skateboarder's travel expenses and equipment. Some skaters earn enough money from their sponsors to make a living just from skateboarding.

Apryl
Woodcock

25

CHAPTER FIVE

PRO SKATERS

Today's female skateboarders are putting lots of energy into their sport. They're excited about what they do and always work to take their talent to the next level. Here are some women to watch:

A neighborhood friend with a skateboard got Mimi Knoop interested in the sport. There were only a handful of skateboarders at her school when she was growing up, and they were all boys. But Mimi didn't let that stop her. She skated her way to three X Games medals.

Mimi Knoop

CB Burnside

Words like legendary and pioneer are often used when Cara-Beth Burnside's name is mentioned. She goes by CB, and got into skateboarding after a skatepark opened near her house when she was a kid. She paved the way for pro girl skateboarders when she started competing against the guys in the early 1990s. As more girls got into the sport, she began winning women's contests. She's won many X Games medals. Tricks like judo airs and inverts consistently awe her peers.

A native of Fort Myers, Florida, Elissa Steamer started skateboarding when she was 12. Her specialty is street skating. Elissa won the first women's street contest at the Slam City Jam. She was voted "Female Skater of the Year" in 2003 by *Check It Out* magazine. You can even step into Elissa's skateboard shoes—she's one of the skateboarders on the Tony Hawk video games.

Elissa Steamer

Lyn-Z Adams Hawkins realized she loved skateboarding when she was 11. When her brother broke his ankle, she either had to head to the skatepark by herself or stay home. She loved skateboarding too much to sit around at home, so she took off for the skatepark.

The California native is known for her handplants and kickflip indies. She's won two X Games medals. "I like skateboarding because it's a really independent sport," she says, "but at the same time you do it with all your friends."

Lyn-Z Adams Hawkins

There's no straight path to the top of the skateboarding world. But one thing's certain: skateboarders do it because they love it. If you love to skateboard, your enthusiasm will come through. Keep riding and one day you could become one of the best!

GLOSSARY

air (AIR)—to get all four wheels off the ramp or bowl

deck (DEK)—the wooden part of a skateboard

dropping in (DROP-ing IN)—entering a bowl or vert ramp from the top edge

grind (GRINDE)—to ride on the board's trucks on the edge of an obstacle

kickflip (KIK-flip)—a trick in which the skater flips the board over during an ollie

ollie (AH-lee)—a trick in which the skater steps on the back of the board to make the board rise into the air

truck (TRUHK)—a piece on the bottom of the deck that holds the wheels on a skateboard

FAST FACTS

 In the early days of skateboarding, the sport was called sidewalk surfing.

 The ollie was invented by Allen "Ollie" Gelfand in 1978.

 Women were first invited to skateboard at the X Games in 2003.

READ MORE

Miller, Connie Colwell. *Skateboarding Big Air.* X Games. Mankato, Minn.: Capstone Press, 2008.

Morgan, Jed. *Skateboarding.* No Limits. North Mankato, Minn.: Smart Apple Media, 2006.

Segovia, Patty, and Rebecca Heller. *Skater Girl: A Girl's Guide to Skateboarding.* Chanhassen, Minn.: Child's World, 2006.

INTERNET SITES

FactHound offers a safe, fun way to find Internet sites related to this book. All of the sites on FactHound have been researched by our staff.

Here's how:

1. Visit *www.facthound.com*

2. Choose your grade level.

3. Type in this book ID **1429601345** for age-appropriate sites. You may also browse subjects by clicking on letters, or by clicking on pictures and words.

4. Click on the **Fetch It** button.

Facthound will fetch the best sites for you!

ABOUT THE AUTHOR

Terri Dougherty has written more than 50 books for children and teens. She lives in Wisconsin with her husband and three children, who provide her with daily inspiration for her writing. She's enjoyed writing about sports like karate, paintball, and, of course, skateboarding. She also writes about a variety of topics as a newspaper reporter. In her free time she plays soccer and skis. And she still has the bright yellow skateboard she rode around the driveway when she was a kid.

INDEX

J
796.220
D

SEP   2007

Dougherty, Terri

Girl's Skateboarding.

$18.95